Pawprints and Moonlight

Sywen Feuerstein

Presentation by *BookLeaf Publishing*

Web: www.bookleafpub.com

E-mail: info@bookleafpub.com

ISBN: 9789357618038

First edition 2022

*To the family and friends who have stood by me
through thick and thin*

*Even when I wasn't cooking with all my
marbles*

PREFACE

As long as I can remember I have loved poetry. From collections like A Children's Book of Verse, read aloud to me as a tiny person; to the Beatnik poems of the '50s and 60s, with a special cadence all their own; to classics found in books with old cracked leather bindings, smelling of that vanilla adjacent aroma that can only be called Old Book. When they taught us about poetry in school it was absolutely liberating. So much room to move, no format and yet so much individual form, lines evoking pictures and inspiring creative punctuation. No matter how many stories or letters to no one in particular I may have written, it's poetry that I wake up to write in the middle of the night.

The Story

The music has stopped but the dancers keep
swaying, the lights have gone out so they dance
by the moon
The chair in the corner lies empty and dusty for
warmth of the covers and lovers in bloom
They stood by the wayside and counted the
corners, the corners in stops gos and stages
between
They found the first fork and they stood in
between it, decisions too great for all that's
unseen
We wait in a room for the answers to find us, no
contact four walls and no comfort around
We took doors for granted as decorative
gestures, until one was opened and answers were
found
A gentle persuasion, no more than a whisper,
crepe paper ornament flowers in full bloom
They withstood the pounding and weight of the
ages, once more to be lit by the light of the
moon

A World in My Back Pocket

There is a world in my back pocket. There is a
world in my back pocket of hoping and
dreaming, mixed in with lint balls and crumpled
up pieces of
receipts on redemption and chlorine for my soul.
  I must admit that when I saw you I put you
there
tucked you away amongst my imagined
palisades
created that world full of daytime dreams for
tomorrow and yesteryear

                        do you like it here?
There's a world in my back pocket
A world you'll never see, but for the fiction of
you
Molded from the outside in and stuffed with
sawdust and fantasies,
      You live there now
sheltered away from my glow for you.
Insulated from anxiety and impulse by layers of
the finest denial cotton
        I can weave wonders for us there
Spun from daylight filtering lazily through a
thousand thoughts

           catching on possibilities

And when the sun at last has set
I sleep
hang up my world to catch new wishes that fly
off in the night

and dream.

Dance

Dance.
One, two, drop step, shake
                because the music is high,
high like wind like spirit like bodies in mind like
the ride that rides the body from the drop beat til
the beats drops and the feet skip the trip until
there's nothing left but the
One, two, drop step, shake
                and spin, arms tight coiled
for spring fingers outward, to unwind the
binding air from the unhindered lungs body,
mind, soul, spirit, wind
Wind, winding, spiraling, careening and
preening. Body to body to body to toe to toe to
cheek to cheek to torso heart thumping to the off
beat almost losing it's own beat to the intent new
beat thrumming.
That thump begins to pump the blood to the
bump, bump, slide,
wait…
wait..
wait.
heaving til the shoulders squirm like the breath
just needs to break out break loose break free,
free,

Free like bird's flight traced in strands of hair,
eyes passage and trailing fingertips. Till the beat
fades, beat fades, going like there's no going,
going, gone,
split second eye to eye to eye to whirlwind
mind.

The Ghost of Lovers Past

In the absence of a Someone, I am haunted
By the ghost of lovers past
An amalgam I have stitched together
With happiness and dreams
Formed and moulded of all of the best pieces of
every intimate encounter
Intimate
Knowing
The barest touch of skin on skin
The way his hands held my hips
Using my hip bones like handholds
To hold love close
To make love stay
Her breath on my cheek
The feel of two hearts beating in time
His chest pressed to my back as he held me
    Little spoon
Tucked away from the world that would intrude
on our…

Loneliness
Because the trouble with such a ghost is that
For all the memories
They cannot love you back
Their essence empty of presence as

They practice the actions of love...

...ing

The caress in passing
The kiss
Stolen as I cook
Because they couldn't wait another moment
For the touch of lip pressed to lip
Breath shared in the spaces before
And after
Or for that nibble snuck from the pan while I
was too busy smiling to care

But these actions are acted out in past tense and
shadows
And though my imagination may be so
Vivid
I can almost feel rough calluses against my
cheek
Almost see the smiles that rouse flurries of
butterflies
Almost hear the voice whispering sweet
nothings
And everythings
And all of the nonsense in between into the
curling shell of waiting ears
Almost
Almost
All-most is nowhere near close enough
To be satiating

To be satisfying
To be love
To being loved
To loving
To being real

I am a person of simple intimacies
A smile across the room
A touch
A voice softening with care
Intensifying with urgency
And no matter how I cherish the memory
Stitching it together carefully with happiness
and dreams
Constructing wistfully my ghost from the
shadows of lovers past
The ghost cannot dance with me in the kitchen at
midnight
Cannot hug me so tight I might fall to pieces
    Or perhaps be put back together again
Cannot change
    And age
    And blossom with me as I grow
Because the evolution of a ghost of lovers past
Is through heartbreak and renewed solitude
Is through the application of new memories
New instances of lovers gone
Stitched into place with the aching memory
Of happiness and dreams

A Tale of the City

Plastic grocery bags float
Like urban tumbleweeds

Through city parks and down abandoned streets

Hopping passing breezes it

Hitchhikes from Wall Street to Harlem where
Street lamps glow with evening magic

And even the rats move to the concrete
embedded spirit
Of half-remembered jazz

They flow with the imprints of innumerable
forgotten fingerprints
And the dance continues under intermittent
spotlight

Several Thousand Mile Kisses

Sending several thousand mile kisses
I am sending several thousand mile kisses
Crossing continents at the speed of cell phone
Redirection and reroute through
Three states south, skipping over balding
farmers and pausing for Rockwell paintings
Sharing pie with lonely diner occupants and
loving the earth
Redirection and reroute from the lips
Kisses sent through finger tips
Playing lightly across keys to fire the receiver's
synapse with longing
Give me everything
I want to know everything
Send me the world in several thousand mile
kisses

My Own Personal Tap Dance

I got my suits my masks and my own personal
tap dance
I lay me down at night and strip me of my
posturings that would make it seem alright or
make me more capable at least
I lay down and sigh
I lay me down to cry
I lay me down in the hopes that today will pass
into tomorrow and it's specter will leave the hell
alone so I can walk my bare feet down unclean
streets without care for yester-somethings that
would wish me my tomorrow's fear
I got my suits my masks and my own personal
tapdance
I wake me up dress me up make me up and
dance my confidence out onto city streets what
light up like stars so wonderers and wanderers
won't know the difference
No stars shine in black and blue sky
I wake me up dress me up make me up place my
mask securely before my features and tell you
it's okay
Patience of a Saint I paint on my lips to say that
transgressions of the past have been forgotten
and the future is a hand yet dealt for you to win

Win
Win
I wake me up dress me up make me up don my
suit to disguise my mind and hold hands out
lovingly
Decorating them with welcome that trails to
safety in my arms
I wake me up dress me up make me up pull my
mask down over mouth like a filter
Paint the door that opens into my rage and pour
through softened words on straight paths
Woulds
Coulds
Shoulds
And mayhaps…
I got my suits. my masks. and my own personal
tap dance
At times fit so tightly
that it's only by removing them that I
                                breathe
As I pull my sheets up over my first suit that fits
my bones best, let the lights out on the face my
parents made me, find myself my stillness
And leave me

Night Connections

Cool cats wait silent under solitary street lamps, wearing smoke like an overcoat two sizes large. the too bright cherry speaking back in the language of tail lights and stop signs warning passers by of toxicity, or is it just proximity? interchangeable these days, like coal dust for sleep: leaving dark eye shadows somehow more visible in moonlight. These cool cats they wait, wait under solitary lamp lights for slick chicks and dames with no better time than night times and shady hours spent any way but lonely; cause loneliness is death to the hypervigilant and chronic need is harder to ignore than chronic pain. Hands reaching for another fix, fixating on contact, the warm pulse beneath soft skin narcotic, cool cats and slick chicks colliding, providing, dividing and careening off down the road for the next easy pickin's. rain slicks the street like gasoline, greasing the bright from the ground up and lending devils halos dirt cheap, no interest.

A Nightingale's Song

The song was joy unadulterated
Spread wingtip to wingtip and fluttering
Rejoicing in it's freedom
confined neither by tempo nor bars

The song was joy exalted
The little nightingale sang it unreserved and
drew ear after ear with its abandon
And what entered the ear drifted through the
mind
Twisting joy into longing
Coveting it's freedom
Confined by neither tempo nor bars

The song was joy incarnate
That inspired uplifted fingertips in invitation
A pleasant perch that extended to a gilded cage
At first a wonder to be explored
Unnoticed the denial of freedom
Confined not by tempo but bars

The song was joy encapsuled
So foreign it required closer examination

To be captured, quantified, and reproduce the
trills and warbles that so enthralled
Ever reducing the little bird's freedom
Confined within tempo and bars

The song was joy remembered
And it dwindled with the passage of metronome
marked seconds
Wingtips no longer catching playful breeze
The nightingale languished
So close but so far from freedom
Confined by both tempo and bars

The song was joy
But the captive bird no longer sang
It's coos awakened with mourning
Silence noted
gentle hands brought nightingale to sprouting
branch
Returning to the bird It's freedom
Far from tempo and released from bars

And the song was joy
High flying and wheeling with new life
Spread wingtip to wingtip and fluttering
Rejoicing in newfound freedom

Messages

The ancient trees, though they hide their faces
from gossiping squirrels through the height of
the day, peek at us and whisper in darkness
The stars twinkle in their branches as they
crinkle leaves in thought, holding forth in
languages we no longer understand on the
goings on beneath their shaded arms.
The wind carries their words to the sleeping
birds, painting their dreams with oak and willow
and imparting messages for them to sing to us
with the rising of the sun.

1...2...3...20

1...2...3...20
I am without words
I am walking
I am
Dancing
I am crying out salutations to the sun
My feet pound against bare pavement and are
grabbed by the waking sky
1...2...3...20
My toes spread and form
New mountains in sand
Hinting at labyrinthine tunnels
Anthills without foundation
Only to be swept wild as
My heels kick
New Stars into the daytime sky
Hanging on a breeze to descend on unfamiliar
inches of waiting earth
1...2...3...20
Thistles bleed my toes
Hidden in stillness among less aggressive blades
of grass
My ankles brushing on a microcosm of wildness
My legs stretching upwards towards tree line
And extending, flowing to the center of the earth

1…2…3…20
My feet pound against bare asphalt
Reshaping the world in my wake
Picking up the taste of the city
And
Never
Falter

If...

If she could be said to dance through life
It was not because she did not carry the weight
of worlds across her shoulders
It was because her movements seemed to sway
to the melody of otherwise unheard music
If she could be said to breeze through life
It was not because she never encountered
barriers or snares
It was because she followed her breath from
moment to moment riding the contraction and
release over, around, and through
If she could be said to exist as a child at play
It was not because the aging of her body never
touched her or she was unmoved by severity
It was because life was too precious to allow the
serious to outshine the ridiculous, the joyous,
and the moments of wonder
If she could be said to be freewheeling
It was not because she lacked regard for the
letter and the law
It was because sometimes the status quo left one
stuck in the mud and when carrying forward
movement momentum is preferable to muscle
If she could be said to dance through life

It was the culmination of a million moments
where the internal music had stopped
Breath faltered
severity set in
momentum faded
And it took every ounce of effort to resume the
dance in the void
If she could be said to dance through life it was a
triumph of obstinate delight

Sudden Showers

Raindrops tap-dance on passing umbrellas
Beating a tattoo above sheltered heads
Sliding silently across stretched fabric as they
succumb to the inevitable call of gravity
Chording and twisting
Separating into beads and streams
Singing lyrics in morse code to the waiting earth
below
Inspiring poetic blossoming
      Orchestrating tributaries
            beyond the curb
               and saturating
                 unprepared shoes

                   to the toes

The Huntress

Somewhere in her memory she knows what I
know
With some ancient bone deep knowledge
Passed on from a time before her ancestors
began to play at domestication
Instincts that enact themselves across her
domain of urban security
A grocery bag hunter
Intolerant to dirt between her toes
A hedonistic beauty
Fiercely protective of her personal space
Easily distracted by stray fibers and
unsuspecting plush toys
She admires the freedom of birds through panes
of glass
More conditioned to comfort and easy excess
Than the genuine urge for survival
Despite diminutive stature she is an ambush
predator
Covetous eyes focus and refocus
Peering out from the clutter on my kitchen table
She stalks my breakfast in silence

Smile

Upon smiling as some men tend to smile in the
company of women
His mouth tilted as is customary
Within the bounds of acceptable angles
Tried and tested
Socially approved
Designed to please with carefully constructed
geometry
Gently involving the cheeks
And causing rather becoming indentations
                              barely hinting at
dimples
As the lip may be allowed to quiver with implied
amusement
An amusement in which the chin declines to
take part
The smile charming
as if to say
I could dazzle too, you know
                    If I felt like it
Yet, when he smiled as a boy will many times
smile
Before the face learns to contain its joy
The corners of his lips would dive recklessly
Spanning his face at skewed angles and

Building pillow forts under his eyes
As if blushingly attempting to hide under those
cheeks
                         that earlier so deftly hid
their fullness
Unpracticed and with only natural grace
Enthusiasm evident in dimples for days
Laughter is barely contained
                         chin wobbling
If it hasn't erupted from the chest and spilled
over the edges of that Smile
Clearly
   I can dazzle too, you know

In the Beginning

In the beginning in the beginning in the
beginning I want to wrap myself up in all of the
beginning because the beginning is always best,
in the beginning we talked like we had more
than words tumbling blithely from over-active
lips that only really wanted to know one another
mentally spiritually physically but in the end it
was I that held back and you that would not
begin so we spoke, and in the beginning in the
beginning in the beginning we were the only
people in a crowded room in the beginning and
we never saw anyone but for when we chose it
and in the beginning we laughed our laughs
bubbling up and dancing off on winds like tides
that ebbed and flowed from somewhere behind
the esophagus rumbling in stomachs and
co-mingling in the space between the space
between beginnings because there are so many
beginnings, in the beginning I was brought by a
stork from some fairytale kingdom and it
dropped me in my mother's lap on the
over-white bed sheets aesthetically patterned
with blood to prove that we're all really from
inside down there or in the beginning there was

a man and a woman who loved on another very
very much and had intercourse and from that
intercourse one very lucky little sperm managed
not to die in the harsh habitat that is the female
reproductive system and found its way to a
lovely pink egg that looks kind of like a pearl or
at least that's how all the picture books showed
it and it said "Hey Baby, what's happening" and
with little thought or regard for the egg's
personal comfort it plunged itself into the egg's
center and that created me myself and I when the
DNA mixed itself up and began to slowly form a
fetus but not so slowly if you think about the
fact that I have all ten of my fingers and all ten
of my admittedly small toes and all of the
internals and externals that make up my
physiology and, well that's a lot to have happen
in only nine months, in the beginning there was
a little girl with a paintbrush and she made
herself a world of paper and color creating new
images of lost memories and passion on pages
that Mommy and Daddy never thought were
finished but hung on the fridge just the same, in
the beginning I never thought I'd fall in love
with someone like you in the beginning I never
thought I'd fall for anyone like anyone I've
fallen for because I didn't know what falling for
someone was until I tripped one day and found
myself interested in ways that surprised my child

self who could only conceptualize a fairytale,
because in the beginning I was shiny and new
and loud for my quietness and big for my
littleness and given to losing myself in other
people's stories without a map to return to this
real real realness and beyond everything else
what we made was real in the beginning of the
beginning of the beginning laughs tangible and
full of sweetness hands touching arms holding
and embrace so real it was hard to let go and in
the beginning I didn't know who I would meet
as I stood on a street corner wanting to be seen
and heard and to take up space in a way I had no
words for and could not ask you to see because
when the beginning had slipped away I began all
over again embracing even more beginnings
until I finally understood that from the beginning
it was my very own self that I needed to shape
me.

Complications

Hands moving with orderly precision
Ticked off in seconds
In minutes
In hours
The view so soothing and simple we don't
always remember
Complications
Spinning
Interlocking
Pressure passing piece to piece
Tension moving in meticulous order
Time piece marking the progression of time

Progress
From complications

Without which time stops
Hands halt
A stillness almost deafening

Therein the hidden virtue of unexpected
complications

Balance

She is a being of ancient waters and earth
these are the greater part of her
When balancing four elements within the self
Even the air of her is not in stillness
nor the winds of the stratosphere
or the hot breath bearing down from the sun
but rather
the leaf spinning in the breeze
the dancing winds across the oceans
the echoing hiss of the caverns respiratory
system
stirring the tiny hairs on bats wings
When the fire of her is lit
it is more akin to the fire of lightning in the
downpour
striking quickly
and where it inspires the blaze it is soon
drenched
reduced to the char that marks its passing.
Her passions run deep as ocean currents
The unsuspecting might be lost
Lacking the wherewithal to navigate its pull
She is a thing of ancient waters and earth
She is drawn to the fire and air of others
but they are not alike

they do not see the patterns of the dance in the
same colors and
so she acts in balance
so much so that
she sometimes fears
that she will be burned from the inside out
and cast adrift on the wind.

A Tale of The City (2)

Evening breezes reshape themselves
Flowing through the city as the sun finds it's
resting place

Floating down side streets
They trade clandestine leaves on corners

Converging on avenues in discarded whirlwinds
And forming great rivers of ghostly breath

Mischievously lifting skirts and swiping loose
hats
Tousling hair and whispering new shapes into
being

Learning the landscape and beauty
Of a thousand faces in passing

Highway at Midnight

The road stretches off into oblivion by cover of
night
As though extending through some ancient
abyssal plain
Populated by floating lights twinkling with the
outlines of cities
Drawing a fairyland by the same token that
clouds draw unicorns

The highway holds its own gravity
     Rubber to road
holding tightly to this pocket of headlight and
rolling us in isolation along its painted surface
This bubble of illumination marks the scant
distance from drowning in potential starlight
And
We could be
      anywhere
      We could be doing loop-de-loops and
flying through
      nowhere
  imagining the silhouettes of trees to keep us
firmly connected to the ground
Would I be so certain of my position
Without a target in mind?

Riding the tightrope between journey's start and
journey's end
The winding line between hither and yon
securing me to the map's face and building
parameters for this headlong careening into
shadow

Would I fly freely through the spaces between
with no sense of safe haven

Without space
Without time
Without
A destination on the other side of the darkness

The Living Tree

That solitary tree stood through the storm
It's roots digging deep through layers upon
layers of ages and loam
It's branches reaching up beyond the heavens
and through planes of existence inviting
ancestors to enjoy the shade when the sun is
high, the fruit when the bough is heavy, the
warmth of It's kindling when stray branches and
leaves begin to fall
The solitary tree stood through the storm
The bark neither rough nor smooth
The leaves neither smooth nor serrated
On those days when it's branches exploded into
bloom it was with unpredictable flowers
Continuity of shade and shape meaningless in
the dazzling array
The tree was every tree
And no tree at all
And it stood through the storm
Undaunted
Melding the memory into it's bark and creating
new rings for experience

www.ingramcontent.com/pod-product-compliance
Lightning Source LLC
LaVergne TN
LVHW010930200726
843509LV00013B/2146